The Wing Chun Forms: Combat Textbooks

Why Wing Chun Works III

Alan Gibson

www.wingchun.org.uk

Printed and bound in Great Britain by Biddles Ltd
www.biddles.co.uk

Published by Summersdale Publishers Ltd
46 West Street, Chichester, West Sussex
PO19 1RP United Kingdom
www.summersdale.com

ISBN 1 84024 375 9

The Wing Chun Forms: Combat Textbooks

Without Whom

Clive Potter and Dave Peterson offered me lots of technical advice, they also both contributed to the text and editing. Ben at Stilsaw.com did the main photography. Dave McCue and Janis Dreosti were models. Kirsteen McKinnon lent us her dummy and performed the form; I photographed this myself with the help of my Parents. Clive Kent designed the jacket, Pete Harvey produced the book, Dave Kerrigan and Mike Wooles added contributions, John McFarlane, Ashley Cooper and Kevin Bell gave proofing and advice. Thanks also go to my brother John for helping me print my last book and my girlfriend Sarah for final proofing and support.

The Wing Chun Forms: Combat Textbooks

Contents

Foreword I

It is once again my pleasure to invite the reader to sample the latest, and most ambitious volume on Wing Chun by my good friend and follower of the Wong Shun Leung Way, Sifu Alan Gibson. As with his first two efforts, Alan has once again managed to capture the essence of the system and has presented it in a manner that is easily understood by the reader, even if they have a limited background in the system.

Where the first two volumes looked at the general theories, techniques, drills and concepts of the Wing Chun system, this time Alan has taken us on a detailed journey through the first two 'empty-hand' forms and the unique Wooden Dummy form. Together, these three forms constitute the basic training methods and combat philosophy of the Wing Chun system. After finishing this book, the reader will not only have a detailed knowledge of the depth of the information contained within the forms, they will also have been inspired to discover ever greater insights into the Wing Chun personal combat system, and have at their disposal, a superb reference to which they will refer to for inspiration again and again. This book is a must for every martial arts library.

David Peterson, Melbourne Chinese Martial Arts Club.

Foreword 2

For those of you whom have read all of Alan's previous books, it is clear to notice his swift development of his Ving Tsun thinking towards the concepts of the way of Wong Shun Leung. I remember Alan once saying to me 'I feel that many persons practising other martial arts would eventually gravitate to Ving Tsun in their search for 'the truth', but once having studied Ving Tsun would then gravitate toward the Wong Shun Leung system as it is logical and makes perfect sense.'

Alan himself has travelled this path, and that is reflected in this book to an even greater extent than the last. To my mind this book is the best he has accomplished to date and well worth reading. I myself started writing a book giving an in-depth analysis of Siu Lin Tau. It was only then that I realised the amount of time and patience needed to write a book such as this. Alan has now done a great job in producing his own book that gives a further insight to the reader as to the thinking and concepts behind the Wong Shun Leung system.

Clive Potter, Wong Shun Leung Ving Tsun Kung Fu Association U.K. Visit www.wongvingtsun.co.uk for more information on Clive Potter and the association.

Introduction

Before we get into this book, I want to clear up a couple of misconceptions about Wing Chun and fighting. Firstly, if you don't want to fight, you rarely actually *have to* (there are normally the options of avoidance or running away). If you don't like fighting, you need to be aware of your environment and sensitive to what is happening around you. If you are threatened, you should then attempt to verbally dissuade the aggressor. If there are no other options and you genuinely feel you cannot escape confrontation, or you are attacked, you must fight and *fight to win* (bearing in mind legality and use of reasonable force).

Secondly, lets remember what Wing Chun is. Wing Chun is a very effective fighting art, a finely honed and efficient weapon. It is not something to use lightly, and when used, the intent is to cause harm, pain and damage. Sparring is a game, played in a controlled environment under the restriction of rules. Fighting has no rules, and in order to survive a fight you will need to attack your enemy and knock them down, or hurt them in order to win.

Thirdly, you don't ever have to get into a fight to profit from training in Wing Chun. There are many positive benefits from practising including: personal development, improved confidence and self-esteem, fitness, health, socialising with people and stress relief, among others. It is, however, wise to remember what Wing Chun was originally intended for, otherwise it is possible to lose focus on how you train.

Finally, if you do like fighting, have to fight often or simply enjoy testing your martial skill then Wing Chun could just be the perfect vehicle for you. I do not teach morality in my classes, because I'm not sure I'm qualified to do so, but I will always try to lead by example. I do not like fighting and will always avoid aggression if I can. You cannot realistically expect to come out of a fight with no injuries at all, although this may happen. Wing Chun will not make you a 'superman'; most real fights are brutal, and over very quickly. Wong Shun Leung used to say, *'Fighting is like playing chess, you have to lose some pieces to win the game. You may have to take a small injury or two to win the fight.'*

Any fight may carry grave consequences. There have been two recent incidences in my home town Southampton, where falling (onto their heads) after one punch has killed people. An argument over a taxi turns into a potential life sentence! Also, if you do win a fight, the loser may hold a grudge (or a weapon) and come back later, or return with reinforcements, or even attack you unawares a month later. Most of the time, however, it is possible to avoid violence, if you are able to communicate effectively whilst not appearing to be intimidated.

The Wing Chun forms are a path to freedom, not restriction. Wong Shun Leung, the great Wing Chun scientist and philosopher, said we must be the masters of our kung fu not slaves to it. The practical applications demonstrated here are only some of the many possible interpretations of the movements in the forms. You can express your skill in any way you wish, and certainly any given action will have more than one functional use or idea attached to it.

The Wing Chun forms (combined with Chi sau practice) teach us fighting skill in an easy to learn and systematic way. They also contain all of the ideas central to the system and many techniques. Often, in the heat of conflict, it is impossible to perform a move in a *correct* way, so we have to improvise. Sometimes it may not even be necessary to perform a movement accurately. Later, we can afford to refer back to the forms and take the time to analyse how we might have performed more efficiently. We can then program in better responses via Chi sau training.

Every single action made in the Wing Chun forms has a reason behind it, and the reason is efficiency. Every part of the system stands up to thorough investigation, interrogation and pressure testing. This is because the technique has been sharpened over many years (and hundreds of fights), by the very wise maxim – *More simple, more direct and more efficient.*

Effective Wing Chun is dependent on a clear understanding of whole-body mechanics. Practising the forms on a daily basis allows us to internalise these mechanics in order for our bodies to move more efficiently, and will also program in the basic movement control patterns. Wing Chun also concerns itself with ideas, as well as specific techniques. It is more useful to keep the interpretation of the forms conceptual, than to tie every movement down with a specific, unchangeable purpose. In Wing Chun we also like to train the most important part of the body, *the brain*.

When explaining to other martial artists why we punch the way we do, or why the stance is like it is, I sometimes ask, 'What are the reasons for the way *you* punch and stand?' It is surprising how often people cannot explain these basic points. Naturally, everyone will follow the style that they think is the best for them, but I always find it surprising when people follow a style without an understanding of the mechanics behind it. Fortunately for me, most Wing Chun practitioners seem to have enquiring minds, and perhaps the fundamental nature of the system draws the inquisitive person to it.

Siu Lim Tao

(Young Idea)

The First form is called Siu Lim Tao, meaning Little Idea or Small Thought; Wong Shun Leung said that the translation should be Young Idea, meaning that this form is the seed from which the individual's system will develop. He described this form as being the alphabet of Wing Chun. So, even when you progress to making *words* in Chum Kiu and then expressing these words as *sentences* in Chi sau, an 'A' is still an 'A' and a 'P' is still a 'P'. Siu Lim Tao contains reference points for many of the basic techniques and concepts, so make sure you get it right from the outset.

Siu Lim Tao is made up of techniques with direct application, techniques designed to elicit expanded applications, techniques performed to develop concepts, and techniques designed to load responses into the neural system, shades of grey, not just black and white. Initially, it is more important to understand the ideas behind the system than the techniques.

The form is split into three sections with a different emphasis on each, but the overall aim is to train for a stable stance and structure, develop triangulation and the centreline, and to meditate on the concept of *Lat Sau Jik Chung* (to develop a relentless forward feeling). In every action in Siu Lim Tao, you feel what the elbows are doing.

Any structure needs a strong foundation or it will not stand up under pressure, likewise if you want to hold a conversation you will first need to learn the language. The First form and all the concepts held within it must be fully understood in order for a student to progress successfully. Practising Siu Lim Tao regularly and correctly is the best way to train your body and mind for Wing Chun.

Opening the Stance

The opening shows us how to find the correct stance, defines the Centreline and demonstrates the centre punch. This is in order of importance. First find the stance, then the centreline, then follow with an attack, which is what you would do in a fight.

To open the stance, keep the feet together and bend the knees slightly (losing about 4cm in height). Raise the arms, outstretched elbows pointing down, and then withdraw the elbows to your side (demonstrating the important concept of the wrists being higher than the elbows and shoulders down). Then put your weight on your heels and push your toes out as far as you can sideways. Next transfer your weight to the balls of your feet, and push your heels out until your feet aim to a midway point that would form an equilateral triangle. Now rotate your pelvis forward, clenching the buttocks and drop your torso down until it sits comfortably and lines up with your thighs (here you will lose about 12 cm in height).

It is important to maintain the straight line from the knee to shoulder, as it is essential for whole body movement. Your centre of gravity should be placed over the centre point between your heels; this is the definition of good balance and stability.

The crossed arms then demonstrate and define the Centreline. The first two punches of the form demonstrate correct punching technique, with the relaxed hand being introduced onto the centreline first and being driven down the line by the downward pointing elbow. The knuckles should be rising constantly throughout this action, in order to drive the opponent up and off their stance when you hit them. The punches are followed by a Huen sau wrist stretch, during which the elbow must stay pointing at the floor. In fact *the elbow points to the floor during every action in Siu Lim Tao except Bong sau*. This is to maintain the line of reaction force back into the stance; this makes all our actions powerful and thoroughly grounded.

Section One

The first section promotes the correct exercising of the muscles and joints of the arm and upper body. *Lat sau Jik Chung,* the essential prying / springy force of Tan sau, Wu sau and Fook sau are also introduced (this feeling is also derived from the stance). This section should be performed slowly and naturally, with all movement driven from the elbow. Training for forward feeling, enables us to spring into any gaps in our enemy's defence without thinking or being distracted by any sideways force.

Some people liken this section to Chi Gong training or Tai Chi, but whilst similar benefits can be gained, the emphasis in Wing Chun is always on training effective fighting skills. You should be thinking about or meditating upon the elbow's movement and the body's forward feeling whilst performing this section.

There are actually three distinctly different Tan saus in this form. Thinking about their *action*, as opposed to their *final position* will help to clarify this point. The first Tan sau teaches the prying force; the relaxed hand and wrist is introduced driven by the elbow. The forearm of Tan sau must be perpendicular to the body for it to work properly, even a slight misalignment will allow you to be hit or cause you to defend poorly. Do not allow the angle at the elbow to be too acute by holding the hand too high, or it will be weak.

Pic I *Prying Tan sau*

Pic 1a *Misalignment will allow you to be hit*

Pic 1b *Correct position prevents strike*

Your hand moves out parallel to the ground, and the elbow will rise as it presses the hand forward. The elbow drives the hand forward until the middle finger arrives on the centreline. As the elbow is slowly driven forward its position and feeling is as though it were connected to the hip. As the elbow approaches the front of the body, it attempts to hug the centreline behind the hand. This is difficult at first, but will become easier with practice as the ligaments of the shoulder become more supple and stretched. The movement ends when the elbow reaches a distance from the body of about a fist and a half.

Pic 001c *Tan sau is more powerful at the elbow*

As you perform Huen sau let the elbow relax and move out (in line to move back beneath the shoulder) forming a triangle with the shoulder and centre. In doing this we define the limits within which the elbow works. Now, by bringing the elbow to the side of the body, slowly drag the Wu sau straight back to the chest along the Centreline. Wu sau should always be on the centreline as its purpose is to guard your centre of gravity. The fingers of Wu sau should be relaxed but pointing upwards, the elbow still points to the floor. Wu sau still feels as if it were prying forwards, even though it is travelling backwards due to the angle of the forearm pointing at the opponent's centre of gravity, and it should not collapse if struck from underneath. Wu sau's range of movement in the form also defines the area within which it can safely operate.

Pic 2
Tan sau's strength is derived from this triangle

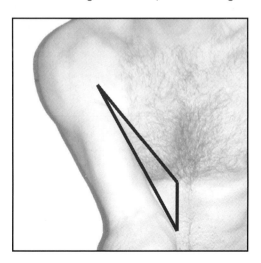

Now the wrist relaxes, and the arm drops into Fook sau. Keeping the wrist slightly higher than the elbow is important for structural strength. The wrist of Fook sau is pushed out down the centreline followed by the elbow. As with Tan sau do not allow the vertical angle at the elbow to be too steep, by holding the hand too high the structure will be weakened allowing your arm to be trapped against your body.

The action of Fook sau and Wu sau is repeated three times, this is because Fook sau is weaker than Tan sau. As it acts from above the arm as opposed to under it Fook sau cannot utilise the upward force of the stance. Therefore we have to train it harder to compensate for this.

The first section closes with Pak sau, a centre palm and the Huen sau stretch: Pak sau, which derives from the Chinese 'to clap' (so now you know the answer to the question, what is the sound of one hand clapping?), is normally achieved from a position of contact. The names in Wing Chun represent actions, not positions and in Wing Chun we do not block but deflect or dispel incoming forces.

Pak sau can be performed from the inside or from the outside. If from the outside you should press the elbow of your opponent towards the opposite shoulder, to further obstruct their movement.

Pak sau on the inside line can be made from above or below the other arm, either way your elbow should simultaneously jam or pin the other elbow of the opponent. The following movement should return the palm to the centre and bring the elbow close to the hip. Then the palm strike should press forwards and upwards along the centre, driven out by the elbow.

Pic 3 *Pak sau from Fook sau arm*

Pic 3a *Followed by a punch*

Section Two

The arms should be relaxed throughout: Often both arms will perform the same move on opposing sides of the body, this has a balancing effect making excessive body movements less likely for the beginner. This section of the form should be performed briskly, but with thinking and feeling behind it.

The side Gum (Soh) sau can also be used to deflect a knee attack. As the knee rises the Gum sau meets the force and the body must pivot or step to deflect the energy. If you try to block a powerful strike head-on, you are likely to injure yourself; the force will travel straight up your arm and damage your shoulder, or at least push you off your stance. It is always better to intercept strikes at an angle and deflect, or push them away. Gum sau moves directly to the target and the turning or stepping of the body moves the limb out of the way.

Pic 4 – 4a *Knee attack deflected with Gum/Soh sau*

In general terms, if the hands are used against kicks, the side Gum sau is used (with a step or pivot) for knees and the front Gum sau for longer-range kicks. It is often more simple to block kicks by shifting stance and attacking with your own feet.

After the left and right Gum sau the elbows move behind the body and jerk upwards, before striking down, and pulling up again.

Pic 5 *Bear hug from behind*

Pic 5b *Jerk elbows up into biceps*

Pic 5a *Move hands behind body*

Pic 5c *Strike down at groin*

Pic 5d *Grab groin and pull*

This action is very effective if you have been grabbed from behind in a bear hug and have your arms pinned down. Jerking the arms upward breaks the grip of your assailant and gives you room to strike down into the groin. From here we can grasp the groin and pull our hands sharply upward and apart. This will be enough to bring tears to the eyes of even the toughest enemy.

Gum sau can also be used if an opponent grabs your wrist and elbow or if an attempt is made to twist your arm into a lock. The action of Gum sau straightens the limb, reducing the available leverage for the enemy to apply a rotating force. You can then place your body weight onto the arm to get rid of the force and counterattack by ramming your opponent with your shoulder or head. The front Gum sau can also be used for blocking kicks.

Pic 6 *Wrist lock attempt*   **Pic 6a** *Straighten arm and push free*

Pic 6b *Step in and shoulder barge*

After performing the front version of Gum sau both arms raise to chest height.

When the arms are whisked out for Fak sau, drop the elbows back and down first to allow the hand to travel in a straight line to the target. The elbow and the hand should also arrive simultaneously for maximum effect, therefore the hands have to travel twice as fast as the arms to arrive at the same time as the elbows. Dropping the elbow (so that it points to the floor) will make the force come from the stance and make the blow far more powerful: You can try this out with a partner.

Fak sau can also be used to remove a pin from the elbow: Bringing the elbow toward the hip deflects the angle of the pinning arm, and spreading the arm will unbalance the enemy as you strike.

Pic 7 *Elbow pinned against body*

Pic 7a *Lever elbow out as in form*

Pic 7b *Strike as Fak sau extends to finish*

The arms then unfold to Gong sau. Notice that the elbows move from a natural position, inwards and forward to deflect an incoming attack. In application your elbow would travel towards the enemy's opposite shoulder as you turn your stance, to clear the way for your strike. This is a very effective technique to use against a shove, often the prelude to further violence.

Pic 8 *Gong sau used to dispel a shove*

Pic 8a *Gong sau used to dispel a shove, note rear hand position*

The forearms then rotate untill the palms point upwards, placing them in a position ready to execute Jut sau. Jut sau is then performed by the elbows being drawn sharply back and slightly down. This is a very strong action and can be used to drag an arm, or even the whole body, off line when used in conjunction with the stance. Some of the best Wing Chun fighters seem to use only Jut sau and punches. Jut sau can be used in conjunction with a punch, if you have been forced out of position, or if your enemy is pressing strongly at you.

Pic 9 *Jut sau against a grab*

Pic 9a *Followed by Biu sau*

After Jut sau the fingers thrust forward into Biu sau. These actions can be used together to intercept an incoming hand and then counter attack, or against a lapel grab (single or double), or they can be used separately.

Pic 9b *It works with two hands too*

Pic 9c *Actually you don't need the Jut sau first!*

The next two actions, pressing the wrists down then up, are used to indicate that in the Wing Chun system the hand always travels in a straight line directly to the target, even if they are extended. Hitting with the back of the wrist is inadvisable, you will know this if you ever played the schoolboy game of knuckles. The upward action can also be used to break a wrist grab, but if you have a free hand it is better to use that to hit with.

These actions are used to reinforce the notion that if the hands or body are poorly positioned (extended in this case) in reference to an incoming attack, rather than trying to turn to face the attack first, the fastest and safest way of intercepting the attack is to move the hands *straight* down, up or across so as to find the closest point of contact. We do not withdraw the elbow first, but rather travel directly to the attack. At that time, with the attack relatively nullified, one can then commence the correction of the posture and positioning and begin the process of counterattack.

As done in Siu Lim Tao, it is a very simplified idea, but the Chum Kiu form applies it perfectly at the end of the third section when the punch is thrown from the lowered left hand as the body is simultaneously squared up. This shows that a diagonal straight line attack is the best method of defence under such conditions. If the opponent's attacking hand is his left, the likelihood is that the limb will be found and can then be used as a bridge to further attacks. If he is unlucky enough to be throwing the attack with his right hand, our direct response will most likely be to hit immediately.

Section Three

The third section, describing the basic actions, opens with Pak sau, side palm (Waang Jeung) and rolling wrist. It goes on to demonstrate Stopping force of Tan sau applications with Jum sau, Lower Gong sau, Huen sau and low palm (Che Jeung), Bong sau with Shifting Tan sau and Toc sau or heel palm (Dai Jeung), then finally, two arms working together to recover from a compromised position. This section should be practised with an emphasis on correct positions and use of elbow energy. The form closes with a series of rapid punches and Huen sau.

As mentioned previously Pak sau can be used from the outside or inside line, and the elbow should pin the other arm simultaneously. After Pak sau the elbow is withdrawn to allow the strike to be made without crossing the arms and to allow the next strike to line up. The palm that is striking will always travel directly to the target, taking the shortest, fastest possible route. The elbow, however, may take a different route in order to deal with varying circumstances. If you attack from the inside, the elbow will stay out to protect the line. If you attack from the outside line, the elbow will move in for the same reason. We can achieve these difficult positions due to the work done in the first section. In short, this section teaches us how to use the elbow to cover the centreline if necessary as you attack.

Pic 10 *Palm strike with elbow covering next attack from outside*

Pic 10a *Palm strike with elbow covering next attack from inside*

Now we introduce the second type of Tan sau, the 'Stopping force', so called because the Tan sau motion does not need to be completed before it can be converted into an attack. Tan sau and a strike can be used on the inside or outside line. However, if you are on the inside line you are vulnerable, because one side of you is open to being hit by the next hand. The example shown in picture set 11 is an outside line Tan sau with a strike, followed by a Gong sau to cover the following low - straight attack. The elbow of lower Gong sau must move straight down to the side of the body. It must not arc outwards, otherwise you will be easily hit.

Pic 11 *Stopping Tan sau*

Pic 11a *Continues to strike*

Pic 11b
*Follow up,
lower Gong sau and hit*

In Wong Shun Leung's Ving Tsun system, there is an extra Tan sau, lower Jum sau and Huen sau in the third section. This change was incorporated as a result of real fighting experiences and here I will pass you over to David Peterson momentarily, to explain the story.

'While fighting a rather stubborn opponent during one of Sifu Wong's many celebrated contests, his opponent, in a fit of desperation and at the point of exhaustion, dropped to one knee and lashed out with a punch which Sifu Wong attempted to deflect with the Jum sau movement contained within his form. Because the attack was so low, the Jum sau only partially deflected the blow, which then struck Wong in the upper thigh, leading to an injury, which nagged him for months. He went on to dispatch his opponent, after which he and Grandmaster Yip got into some heavy discussion about what had transpired.

As a result of this discussion, Yip Man advised his students to include the technique known as Lower Gong sau in place of the Jum sau previously found in this section of the form. Sifu Wong decided that both techniques were important (especially in view of the fact that the Jum sau is an integral part of the basic single sticking hands, and so continued to include both, while most, if not all of his classmates (the *instructors of today) dropped the 'old' technique in favour of the 'new' one.*

Grandmaster Yip Man had explained to Sifu Wong that the Jum sau movement had been taught to him by Leung Bik, his second teacher, who had been a very small man and had not needed to make much use of the lower action Lower Gong sau. Chan Wa Sun, on the other hand, being a taller man, would often make use of the lower action as many of his opponents had been smaller than himself, and therefore were more likely to hit lower. Grandmaster Yip, being more influenced by his second teacher, Leung Bik, had therefore altered his form accordingly. Jum sau is also a much more subtle action than the Lower Gong sau movement and therefore less likely to be included in the arsenal of a man like Chan who tended to just blast his opponents out of his way.'

Excerpt taken from 'Look Beyond the Pointing Finger – The Combat Philosophy of Wong Shun Leung' by Dave Peterson

The next demonstration shows one way in which the lower Gong sau could be used, as the opponent steps round and tries to deliver a low hook or uppercut to the floating rib area after a wrong Bong sau has been used.

Huen sau is used extensively in the Siu Lim Tao form. When the arm is held straight the action is a wrist stretch and strengthening exercise, in the third section we look at the action in use.

Pic 12 *Wrong Bong leaves you vulnerable to attack*

Pic 12 *Wrong Bong - Gong sau*

Huen sau has many applications, although it is rarely used in fighting. One common, practical application is to change to the other side of an arm or body if we have made a mistake. Huen sau is a very powerful tool when used close in and with the elbow held down. If the elbow lifts you will be hit.

The example shown here illustrates an escape using Huen sau after having used the wrong Gong sau (leaving your right side open to attack). The action will change the angle from one of vulnerability to one of superiority.

Pic 13 *Wrong Gong leaves you open to attack*

Pic 13a *Wrong Gong – Huen sau (and punch)*

The next technique is Bong sau with 'Shifting' Tan sau. This is the third type of Tan sau in Siu Lim Tao. Shifting Tan sau is often used to get rid of, or move around, any rigid pressure jamming our forward movement, as often occurs in Chi sau or in fighting when someone panics and becomes tense.

Pic 14 *If your arm is deflected or jammed on line*

Pic 14a *Use Shifting Tan to evade the force and continue to the target*

The final movement in this form can be used to illustrate three different concepts. The idea demonstrated here is that we should not leave both our arms (elbows) forward or crossed. In other words, as we use our forward arm to deflect an attack, the rear arm should be lining up to hit. As we hit from the rear arm, the other arm must be retrieved to line up for the next strike (otherwise both arms can be trapped). This technique is not for *sweeping* a grabbing hand away. If you are grabbed and have a free hand, you should punch your assailant while they hold you.

Pic 15 *Bong sau used to deflect an attack*

Pic 15a *Do not punch over your Bong sau*

Pic 15b
*Jut or Lap sau
could be used
to trap both your arms*

The last flurry of punches in Siu Lim Tao is there to remind us that one of the best ways to knock out or injure someone is to hit them repetitively in the same place. This concept is known as 'targeting'. If there is too much time between blows the brain has time to recover. If you strike whilst the brain is against the skull, due to a previous punch, you will render your enemy unconscious easily.

There is also another concept in this section and that is that the retreating hand travels back with the same speed and power as the hand going out to punch. Thus both hands arrive at the same time and the forces are balanced. Yin and Yang! It is a common problem that students bring back the retreating hand slower than the one going out which they are concentrating on, thus the other hand is not in position to guard or execute the next action straight away.

Chum Kiu

(Searching For, Building, or Crossing the Bridge)

Siu Lim Tao demonstrates the basic reference points in the Wing Chun structure. Chum Kiu (searching for, building, or crossing the bridge) trains us to maintain these points whilst fighting a moving target or multiple opponents. Basic footwork is demonstrated, but more sophisticated footwork is shown in the dummy. Again the form can be split into three sections, making it easier to understand, but the purpose of each section is not so specific.

Section One

Generally the first section teaches us about tracking and hitting moving targets, and how to turn our stance. It introduces rising elbow strikes, turning on the spot, Lap sau, and Tok sau (Dai Jeung). Bong sau is in contact and on the correct line. The change from Bong to Lan sau with correct elbow positioning is also introduced.

The stance is opened in the same way as in Siu Lim Tao; find the stance, find the centreline, and punch down it. After the punches Gong Sau is introduced followed by a double eye gouge. Needless to say the thumb in the eye is a very simple, yet effective way of dissuading someone from continuing to attack you.

This attack can be performed after a basic palm strike. It is better to use the eye furthest away from you (trapping your opponent's head with your hand) to prevent their simply moving away. Of course this method does not require any stance to deliver, so it will work whatever position you are in.

Pic 16 *The Eye Gouge, simple and effective*

Pic 16a *Works when lifted up from floor*

Pic 16b *Or when pinned on the ground*

The first turn to the left is to practise the rising elbow strike Pei Jaang or Hacking elbows; the following turns are to practise turning on the centre of gravity only. The fast and stable pivot is very important in Wing Chun so make sure you get it right.

The action of Pei Jaang is also excellent as a means of locking up an opponent's arms and putting them out of position. Much of Chum Kiu can be directly applied to Chi Sau. Here there is a direct application to Chi sau, where if when rolling, you feel your opponent forcing your Fook sau off centre with their Tan sau, the Pei Jaang action is created by converting the Bong sau into a grabbing action, taking control of the offending Tan sau and simultaneously pinning the opponent's Fook sau with the elbow which is driven towards their opposite shoulder. When done in conjunction with the pivot, just as in the form, the opponent winds up off balance and completely trapped and you have a free left hand to 'negotiate' with. This is very much like the action of inside Pak sau.

Pic 17 *Your elbow controls the enemy's elbow, while your hand controls their Tan sau*

When pivoting the movement should involve the whole body. The shoulders, hips and legs should move as a single unit. As you reach 45 degrees the legs and hips fix themselves and stop in a strong position. The shoulders stop at 90-degrees to your base line. When turning back, the shoulders move until they are above the hips. They then join and carry on as a single unit, giving whole-body power.

Pic 18 *Begin to turn the upper body from the waist*

Pic 18a *When the shoulders line up with the hips*

Pic 18b *Move the whole unit together*

Next, the arms unfold into Lap sau (Chum Kiu Fook Sau), demonstrating that this action should be performed as one movement.

The forearms now rotate and Tok sau (Dai Jeung) with Jut sau is performed three times (referred to as Jeet sau or snapping / breaking hand). This is a great way of wrenching someone's elbow if they have over committed a technique or reached over in order to hit. It can be used simply to control an enemy by lifting them off their stance. This 'Jeet sau', like the eye gouge, is very dependent on using the correct side, otherwise the opponent will easily escape being damaged or controlled by simply bending the elbow.

Pic 19 *Tok used against over-extended punch*

Thus, if it is the right arm we are controlling, our left arm must do the Dai Jeung action while the right arm does the Jut Sau, and vice versa.

Three palm strikes are now performed followed by a turn to Lan sau. These palm strikes (Jing Jeung) are done across the line of the body. The right palm strikes in the direction of a position in front of the left shoulder, while the left palm strikes towards a position directly in front of the right shoulder. This is an abstract way of reminding ourselves of the key concept of the Chum Kiu form, how to hit a moving target, whereas the Siu Lim Tao form assumes a stationary target for ease of learning. By shooting at targets across the line of the body as described, we are being taught to use the elbows as the targeting device, instead of always turning to face the target first. If not, we will always be a step behind the target.

The position of Lan sau is crucial. It should be at 90 degrees to your enemy, with the elbow held low and the fingers pointing upwards. If someone applies pressure across your arm, for instance leaning on your Bong sau or using Gong sau against your punch, you can drag them in using Lan sau. The Lan sau is now left in a perfect position to shoot forwards and upwards into the waiting chin of your opponent.

Pic 20 *Pressure felt across centre from the outside*

Pic 20a *Pivot to Lan sau to dispel force and draw enemy in*

Pic 20b *Lan sau arm is now on line to attack*

The first Bong sau of Chum Kiu is in contact with the enemy's limb. This is known as Yi Bong, which implies that contact already exists and the opponent's force is being 'borrowed' to drive the technique. The body rotates on the spot and Bong drives across the incoming attack towards the opponent's opposite shoulder, bouncing the elbow of your attacker, using your own elbow, towards his opposite shoulder. This opens the line for attack from you rear hand, which is lying in wait on the Centreline.

There are three important lines in Bong sau, and you will notice that the angle and shape of Bong sau is exactly the same in Chum Kiu as it is in the First form (relative to your trunk), but that the whole torso is turned.

Pic 20c *Bong sau in Siu Lim Tao*

Pic 20d *Bong sau in Chum Kiu applied*

The third Lan sau is followed by a punch, from the elbow directly to the target and with the elbow dealing with any obstacles. As with the earlier palm strikes, this punch is done across the line of the body towards the opposite shoulder to reinforce the idea of hitting what is essentially a moving target. After performing Fak sau the arm returns directly to the centre, leading from the elbow, to cover the centreline. This is a faster route than leading with the hand if the arm is extended.

Pic 21 *After performing Fak sau the elbow is closer to centre than the hand*

Pic 21a *The elbow returns before the hand, as this is faster*

Pic 21b *Leaving the whole arm on line and ready to attack*

Section Two

The Wing Chun forms should never be considered solely as sequences of movements for fighting opponents, but more as collections of ideas and techniques to be practised in such a way as to prepare both the mind and the body for their individual use within a combat scenario. However, as this book is about application, I have taken the liberty of setting up some of the scenes with more than one opponent (see the following examples), in order to express my ideas.

The second section begins with a turn to 90 degrees with Lan sau, and a kick. Lan sau is kept low to prevent an opponent pushing against it to disrupt your stance. Lan sau here is used to create a barrier, which is rammed into the opponent to prevent them punching. Uprooting power is derived from the rear foot and the enemy is driven back. We now use a kick to close the gap that we have opened up.

If someone simply steps back we can chase them with our stance. The difference here is that we have used Lan sau to push the opponent away therefore this action creates a force in our stance which prevents us from immediately chasing the opponent.

Therefore, a space is created between the enemy and us, so we must bridge this space with a kick before the enemy does. When kicking the Wing Chun practitioner should always try to drive forward in order to close down afterwards.

Pic 22 *Lan sau jams a potential threat*

Pic 22a *Pressure from the stance disrupts the enemy and bounces them away*

Pic 22b *The lifting kick is then used to close the gap to Wing Chun fighting range*

In the next illustrated example we are attacked from the side whilst still in motion. In the form we change the direction of our intent or centreline before our foot hits the ground. Emergency Bong sau (Pau Bong, literally 'throwing' or 'casting' Bong sau) is now used; the elbow is thrown out to intercept the incoming attack. The action is upwards and forwards in one motion so that regardless of the height of the attack (it could be going anywhere from the waist to the head, but it has a common origin at the shoulder), we are giving ourselves a chance of intercepting it to form our bridge, with the whole forearm acting as a shield.

This is then followed with the lowered arms, to demonstrate that the hand was lower than the elbow, which is why we are using Bong sau rather than Gong sau. This out of contact Bong sau is repeated three times. Lateral footwork is used for gaining contact or side stepping under pressure; the Centreline is at 90 degrees to the direction in which you are stepping.

After the last Bong sau, we have to deal with another attack coming from the direction we are moving in. Again the hand attacks the target directly (Chau Kuen or 'whipping punch'), whilst the elbow may take a different route, covering the centreline, to cut out any threat from the incoming arm. This action is often wrongly described as an uppercut punch. It is actually driven forwards, to a

Pic 23 *Emergency Bong sau is thrown out to cover a new attack. Here, the attackers position has been thrown out of line by the Bong sau*

height no greater than the upper chest or chin. This is a structurally more efficient way of attacking the body with a punch than the basic vertical fist action.

Pic 24 *The hand of Bong sau moves in a straight line to attack – the elbow covers the centre on the way*

The vertical 'sun' fist is structurally superior between approximately mid-chest to head level, but loses its effectiveness below this height. At lower levels, the snapping wrist action does not work, so the punch can actually be pushed backwards with strength lost through the elbow. By turning the palm upwards and driving the punch upwards and forwards as described, the entire forearm now compensates for the lost wrist action, once again deflecting the return energy down into the floor, the angle of the forearm now identical to the angle of the lower rear leg.

You can easily test the above theory by placing your vertical fist on a partner's stomach and trying to resist them stepping towards you. You will find that your arm soon collapses backwards, but if you turn the palm upwards and point the elbow downwards on the same angle as the rear lower leg, your opponent will have great difficulty pushing your fist back. This clearly shows that if you utilise this shape, you will hit much harder. So, if going for a body shot, this ensures a more effective strike.

As we turn back into the fray our hand leads the head (Yi Ying sau or shape recovering hand), and then drops to deflect any incoming force to allow us to fight again.

Section Three

The third section shows us the front kick - driven up from the floor *as* you turn, forward footwork with a half step, step together. This demonstrates how to push, using the elbow in conjunction with the stance, without leaning or committing the weight.

The low Bong sau can be used for close body control, or if someone tries to hold both your arms down, you can push them powerfully away using your stance. This section can also be shown as Quan sau (low Bong and Tan sau), which is very useful for preventing a large person from grabbing you in a bear hug. Finally we train a kick to

Pic 25 *Quan sau defence against a bear hug*

where our centreline was before the previous step. This shows us again that it is possible to turn around and kick simultaneously. All the power is driven from the leg that is on the ground, and after the kick we step in, to close down. This is known as the Waang Geuk or horizontal kick, and like the Yi Ying sau, it enables us to make a blind turn or recover from a poor position more safely. Hit or miss, it keeps the opponent at bay until we can safely face them, only this time using the leg rather than the hand. It is only done on the left side in Chum Kiu, but gets a workout on both sides in the Muk Yan Jong form.

Wong Shun Leung often said that the reason it is on the left leg only is because most people are natural right-footers and need to work their weaker side more. He used to joke that he had been doing the kick on his left leg for forty years, yet could still kick far better on his right!

Pics 26 – 26b *Kicking whilst turning and closing down*

Gum sau is used to cover the lower gates, mainly against kicks. Remember the First form here and do not meet the force head on, the hand goes down and then the body turns to move the limb out of the way. Finally punching to cover an exposed gate is demonstrated. Here the hand goes straight to target and the elbow intercepts. The overall theme of Chum Kiu is gaining contact with an opponent, then crossing over the bridge to their centre by virtue of correct positioning and angle.

Pic 27 *Gum (Soh) sau to deflect a knee attack*

Pic 27a *Followed by covering punch, which deflects the next attack*

This sequence is one that has direct application in Chi sau training, in that it shows how to drill the interception of kicks that are thrown during Chi sau practice. In order to kick, the opponent has to transfer the weight to one leg, and if reasonable forward pressure is being utilised, this transfer of weight will be felt. When it is, the Fook sau hand changes into Gum (Soh) sau, thus causing a change in the shape of the opponent's hip structure which neutralises the kick. At the same time the opposite hand (Bong or Tan sau) drops slightly back, like a half-Tan, to monitor the opposite hand and seek a counter.

When the above concept is taken out of Chi sau, we are shown that in close range situations, kicking by the opponent can be neutralised by pressing down on the arms or controlling the elbows, while at longer ranges, the palm can be used to deflect the knee or foot in conjunction with a change in positioning, generally in the form of a pivot or side step.

Muk Yan Jong

(The Wooden Man or Dummy)

Wooden dummy training forms an intrinsic part of the Wing Chun system. Literally translated Muk Yan Jong means a wooden structure. Other styles of Kung fu use dummies to practise against but the Wing Chun dummy and its form is specifically designed to practise and improve Wing Chun fighting skills and footwork. The form has undergone many changes throughout it's history. Although there are many different versions of this form, generally the first five sections are similar.

Training in the wooden dummy form will improve many aspects of skill, especially your ability to move freely around a very strong opponent, arriving in a good position and hitting from a correct stance. Many of the moves are illustrated as recoveries from mistakes, but they can also be interpreted in other ways.

The sequences of actions do not need to follow the order of the form; each action can be seen as a separate move. For this reason, it is good practice to mix up the order, and to be able to move freely around the dummy choosing random techniques as they seem appropriate. You can also train the form with an emphasis on training different attributes of your Wing Chun such as footwork, relaxation, waist-power or angle.

There are, however, two moves that must always be linked. Gum sau must always be followed by Tan sau. This is because after shifting a knee or kick, both bodies will be turned, and the part of your body nearest the enemy, will be the hand that was used to cover the attack. The order of techniques demonstrated in this book is what Wong called the 'normalised form'. If you have learned a different sequence, you should notice many similarities in the technique, if not the order.

The dummy contains many important aspects of Wing Chun footwork whereas Chum Kiu only contains the basics. The change from the forward stance to the (square) horse stance and back, is especially important to understand. The forward stance is only used while moving forward, so if you meet a very powerful or immovable opponent you will need to use your mobility to get around the arms to access the person. The square stance is used as soon as you stop moving forward, in order to allow lateral movement, as this leaves the option of moving in or out, with whichever leg is appropriate.

Always remember that a dummy arm could represent the *right or left* arm of the enemy and whilst some people think the end of the dummy arm could indicate the wrist, it is actually meant to be the elbow. The lower arm represents a low blow this could be a punch, kick or knee. The bottom part of the trunk can represent a leg. Also remember that the dummy is made of wood, not flesh and bone so it will not react in the same way as a person. You need to use your imagination in order to get the best out of dummy training.

It is of course possible to strike and kick the dummy with considerably more force than you could safely use against a partner. It must, however, be pointed out that the purpose of the wooden dummy is not to harden the arms or hands, although it will aid your conditioning.

Wooden Dummy Form Illustrated in back pages

Section I

This section emphasises footwork and successful movement around a strong opponent. Stress must be placed upon the practitioner's ability to arrive solidly, at the correct angle, with the hand shapes positioned comfortably and not cramped. When you move in and strike the dummy everything arrives together, you should hear only one sound not two or three. Remember where centre is as you travel. Do not be over-concerned with striking the trunk at first, it is more important to pay attention to your positioning and angle.

The first move is teaching us a concept and is called 'First Contact'. The elbow drives the left hand forward. When the forearm makes contact with the dummy's arm, the elbow force must be trained to continue feeling forward and not to interact with the dummy's arm. After contact is gained, Lap sau is performed with a strike. If this strike misses, and moves beyond it's target (the head), then the same hand is used to sharply tug the head back onto the next incoming punch.

To illustrate how diverse interpretations can be made from this form we will explore several different ways of explaining the following two moves: Bong into Tan sau and strike.

Normal Bong sau (left Bong, right punch) is met with tension or pressure in the attacking arm, so we use a stopping force of Tan sau to move around the force and move in with Tan sau and strike.

Pic 28a 1. *Normal Bong sau is met with pressure from the attacking arm*

Pic 28a 2. *Stopping force of Tan sau is used to get rid of the pressure and attack*

Normal Bong sau is used against a punch, which is quickly followed by a punch off the other arm. We use stopping force of Tan sau to move to the opposite side and strike.

Pic 28b 1. *Normal Bong sau defence*

Pic 28b 2. *Followed quickly by another attack – Stopping force of Tan sau changes sides*

Pic 28b 3. *Allowing a better attack angle*

Wrong Bong sau (left Bong, left punch) is used in an emergency, leaving us vulnerable down the left flank. Stopping Tan sau is used with turn and forward step to correct the error, allowing us to strike centre.

Pic 28c 1. *Wrong Bong sau used*

Pic 28c 2. *Corrected by stepping in with Stopping Tan sau*

If the opponent tries to attack the ribs after we produce a wrong Bong sau, we must use lower Gong sau and strike. Hence the handy saying 'Wrong Bong – Gong'.

Pic 28d 1. *Wrong Bong sau…*

Pic 28d 2. *Gong sau!*

The step through (in example c) is especially important if you are on the inside with a strong puncher. This is because if you just try to pivot, your Tan sau will most likely get squashed sideways and you will be hit. You have to move in, meeting the attack at ninety degrees, before it gains momentum and closes the angle. The same is true from Tan sau and punch on the inside gate.

When training on the dummy you should emphasise the movement after Bong sau (i.e. step out – turn – and step in to attack) for this very reason. Train this footwork with speed and power, and disengage from the dummy arm as you turn the corner. You want to fight the person not the arm.

Pic 29a *(Left) After Tan and palm on the inside, if another attack follows you must step in…*
Pic 29b *Your Tan sau can get crushed up if you just pivot*

The next move is lower Gong sau, combined with a strike and pin (as an opponent tries to step around and deliver a body shot). Again this will work from the outside to the inside or from the inside and staying there. You should not attempt to change from the inside to the outside, or vice versa. Your opponent's movement will dictate your position, your job is to find the shortest route to their centre and attack them.

Quan sau can be used to give you an opening to hit the opponent as you attack. It is possible to run at someone, and hit them with your shoulder as you jam their guard out of the way using Quan sau. This kind of charging attack can be diffused by sharply yanking both limbs to one side.

Pic 30 *Facing off...*

Pic 30a *Quan sau taking guard out…*

Pic 30b *With a shoulder barge*

The Huen and Gong sau, used at the close of each section, is normally seen as a recovery from a wrong Gong sau. Wrong Gong sau leaves us exposed and vulnerable to attack, Huen sau corrects the fault. Hence another nice little ditty, *'Wrong Gong – Huen'*. Huen sau must be performed with the elbow held down; otherwise it will not work if the person is really trying to hit you.

The Huen sau is followed with a Jut sau and strike. Sometimes this strike is sent low, but on a real person (remember the dummy is made of wood!) the Jut sau will jerk the arm down. The strike should always be above the moved arm, otherwise your Jut sau will obstruct your own striking arm.

Pic 31 *When performing Jut sau…*

Pic 31a *You should never obstruct your own low strike…*

Pic 31b *Leaving your enemy with a free hand*

Section 2.

Repeat section 1, starting on the other side.

Section 3

Pak sau is demonstrated here, this can be on the *outside* or *inside* gate depending on how it is performed. Then Jut sau with Fak sau is employed on the outside line. The movement is bounced into a chop and back to another Jut sau with a low strike. Low bong then leads into an unusual inside Fak sau after the attacking hand is stopped with Pak sau. This emergency technique can be handy if you have lost position after performing lower Bong sau.

Pic 32 *Position lost, possibly due to ineffective Bong sau*

Pic 32a *Pak sau recovery*

Pic 32b *Fak sau attack*

Quan sau combined with a side kick, can be used to defend a round kick, although, if your kick is fast enough, your arms will not be needed. The quick side kick is attacking centre as normal. It is often easy to kick the inside of the supporting leg of the kicker. Although I'm not keen on using pressure points, it is useful to note that the femoral nerve is on the inside of the thigh, just above the knee. Put some weight on your leg and strike yourself there, just to see what happens. Ensure that the force from the kick goes into the centre of the dummy and that the foot does not slip off or down the trunk.

Pic 33 *Faced with a kicker on their range.*

Pic 33a Quan sau and side kick used to defend a round kick.

Pic 33b Then close down to Wing Chun range, using the kick as a bridge.

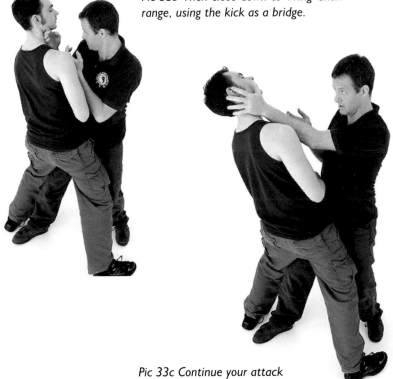

Pic 33c Continue your attack

Section 4

This section starts with a Biu sau movement similar to that found in the opening of the Third form. This can be used if one arm is injured and you need to fight one handed. Next we move into a *wrong* Gong sau, which should be followed by Huen sau to right the positioning.

The next part deals mainly with Po Pai Chung or double palm strikes. Attention must be paid to the position of the opponent's guard. Your strike will be wedging from the inside or outside to trap or jam your opponent, or sometimes freeing your own hand in order to hit.

Pic 34 *Po Pai*

Pic 34a *Po Pai*

These attacks are very powerful strikes, not pushes, and can be used to bounce an enemy into a table or other obstacle such as a wall, a car or a group of your friends.

Also, the lower hand can attack the groin, whilst the upper hand attacks the face or head.

Pic 34b *Po Pai*

Section 5

Thai boxers will often attempt to grasp their opponent's neck with both hands and drag them onto knee attacks. This kind of upright grappling will also happen if an assailant fears that you are getting too close and tries to protect himself. If this happens, you can pike your body backwards whilst pushing (down and out) on the hips. You will need to duck your head down as you do this, to escape the grip.

Pic 35 *Thai Plumb hold*

Pic 35a *Push down and back on hips*

Pic 35b *Keep your head low as you come out*

Gum sau followed by Tan sau is demonstrated next. Gum sau is used with a shift of the body, which supplies the power and deflects the attacking knee. Remember, after shifting a knee, both bodies will be turned, and the part of your body nearest the enemy will be the hand that performed the Gum sau. Tan sau will be needed next to cover any further threat from the enemy as you dispatch them. These two moves are always connected, as mentioned previously (this is also demonstrated in Chum Kiu).

Pic 36 *After using Gum sau to deflect a leg away*

Pic 36a *Your next move should be with the same (closest) hand*

Pic 36b *No matter which hand attacks*

At this point different teachers' forms seem to diverge. This may be according to what actions they deem as being most useful, or just a personal preference to a given order.

Section 6

An attack that drives in and disrupts the opponent's stance is performed. After a low Bong sau to deflect an attack, a stepping movement allows you to access the area behind the lead leg of the opponent and rush in to attack whilst controlling the flank with a pinning hand. The incoming leg will wedge into the knee / thigh area and collapse the stance of your enemy. Pak sau and palm strike are performed simultaneously.

Pic 37 *Stance disrupting attack with pinning hand*

Also illustrated here is the crossed step and recovery kick where the kick is launched off the 'wrong' leg. This kick or sweep is used to recover from being pulled across your own stance. You would not usually cross your own legs deliberately as this leaves the stance vulnerable to pushing and pulling.

Pic 38 *Pulled badly out of position*

Pic 38a *Recovery kick or sweep with grappling hand*

Section 7

The action of Gong sau (upper and lower) is demonstrated initially in this section and repeated three times.

Kicking is again shown here. First a front kick to the hip, or groin area (centre) is delivered in combination with Tok sau to lift the arm/s and break the posture. This is then converted into a nasty shin scrape, used when your Bong sau has been pulled.

Pic 39 *Bong pulled in…*

Pic 39a *Stomp on instep or shin scrape*

The shin scrape is often tricky to perform in practice. Wong Shun Leung taught that it is next to impossible to apply because it is far too natural for the opponent to simply pull the leg away before the action can be completed. He taught this movement as a stomp to the instep as this is very difficult to defend against and very painful in a debilitating way.

This second part of the action can also be used if your foot gets entangled in the clothing of your enemy, or if they grab your leg when you first kick them. You need to bring your weight forward in order to bring your foot back down to the ground.

Pic 40 *A strong shove while unprepared – often the prelude to further violence*

Pic 40a *Tok sau and kick*

Pic 40b *Tok sau also works from a grab, if you don't want to strike*

Pic 40d *If grabbed by one hand*

Pic 40e *Tok sau will work also*

Section 8

The action of Huen sau is demonstrated now, followed by Bong sau pivoting into a Lap sau / Fak sau combination. The concept being illustrated is the control of an incoming force. This can be performed from a deep turn as opposed to a step. The Lap sau (not pulling or pushing, but controlling as you shift your position) is combined with a chop to the throat, and doubled up with a centre palm and Lap sau.

Pic 41 *Bong sau*

Pic 41a *Followed by Lap sau and chop*

The final section concludes the form with two Biu sau moves similar to those found in the opening of the 5th section of the Dummy or in the Third form. It then moves into a straight line (emergency), downward move (similar to the First form after Biu sau). Now you step and turn away slightly, to avoid the incoming attack. The final move of the form is a bridging kick accompanied by Biu sau, used to close the gap between you and your enemy. This was the move often favoured by Wong Shun Leung for closing the initial combat range, during his many successful challenge fights.

Pic 42 *Bridging with a simultaneous kick and eye strike*

Biu Tze

Biu Tze (flying fingers) is the Third form of Wing Chun. The name is derived from characters meaning Moon Pointing Finger, and Wong Shun Leung believed it taught us to 'Look Beyond The Pointing Finger' (see Dave Petersons great book). This is a way of telling practitioners not to be trapped in the standard rules that they have been taught in basic training, and to think outside the box when training or fighting.

The mystery surrounding Biu Tze stems from the fact that it is often only taught to loyal students who have shown themselves to be capable of a high level of development, both through the system and on a personal level. Usually Biu Tze is only taught on a one-to-one basis and a student must certainly have absorbed all the concepts from Siu Lim Tao and Chum Kiu. Frequently it is also considered necessary to study the dummy form before the Third Form. Many of the moves break the Wing Chun rules, coming up from under the bridge or from the 'wrong side' of the body.

Biu Tze form contains many sophisticated ideas, including ways of minimising ones losses if you have been hit, injured or have made a bad mistake during a fight. For this reason it is also sometimes known as the emergency or desperation form. This is one reason for the form not to be shown too early in a person's training. It is better to learn not to make mistakes, than to find ways of correcting them after they have been made. The form is also considered important as it may give clues to potential weaknesses of the Wing Chun system, although it also demonstrates how to overcome these problems.

Hesitation Hurts

By Mike Wooles

The best lists in the world only have three things in them, so that they are easy to remember. With Wing Chun, my three things would be 'Fear is the only enemy', 'Hesitation hurts' and 'I've started so I'll finish!' Here is a short story from my childhood of how I compiled this list.

When I was a kid, I joined a new Secondary School. I was the nerdy new boy, not good at sports, wearing slightly unfashionable glasses and most importantly I was 'not from round here!' While I made plenty of friends in my new school - some of whom became lifelong acquaintances, I was also a target for a few local bullies.

It was mid-afternoon and I was heading from one class to the next and decided to go to my locker to pick up some books. For the umpteenth time that year, M. S. was sitting on top of my locker and grabbed my schoolbag, playing football with it around the locker room. This had been going on for about twelve months now, and although I was a pretty mild mannered kid I was starting to get rather distressed about this.

After five or ten Minutes of being goaded and playing the game, I caught up with M. S. in the corner of the locker room.

He stared me out for a few seconds, enjoying the torment he was inflicting on someone who he considered less able than himself and something inside me snapped. I whacked him in the side of the face with what was probably a right hook. He was stunned. He really hadn't bargained on this today, so I made the most of his shock, grabbed my bag and hightailed it out of the locker-room towards my next lesson. 'Mike 1, Fear 0' today for a change, but as I discovered it was only half-time.

Victory was mine! I had beaten the fear inflicted on me by suffering in silence for all those months, but my celebrations were short-lived. The shock of my blow to his head and his ego had worn off and M. S. soon caught up with me, pinned me against a wall and pummelled me for a few minutes, splitting my lip against my teeth and yelling some abuse. He wasn't a gifted linguist and I can't remember what he said, but your imagination will fill in the blanks. The chap wasn't happy, he hadn't expected to be hit back by the likes of me.

It had taken so much out of me to overcome my fear and hesitation that had held me back for so long, that I had nothing left when it came to the second bout. I was probably so high on adrenalin anyway and wasn't prepared for round two.

I had started so successfully, but hadn't finished what I'd begun. In subsequent encounters, since I have learnt Wing Chun I am no longer scared to stare people down (well, most people), I'm ready to fight if that's what it takes and when its come to a stand-off and gone no further, I've always been very aware for days afterwards that a second round could happen. Its not like the movies where you stride off into the sunset or to your next class at school, you might not make it that far if your opponent is still up for it, so never turn your back until you are sure it is finished.

An Officer Calls

By Dave Kerrigan

Whilst working as a police officer I was called to a house where the occupants were engaged in a violent argument. As luck would have it, I was standing outside the front door as the call came over the radio, so there was no time for me to call for back-up. I knew the family, and also knew the man to be violent and not pleasantly disposed to members of the constabulary! There was nothing for it but to knock on the door.

I was let in by the girlfriend and directed to the garden, where the man was. With sweaty palms and a pounding heart I made my way to the garden. The sight of the man confronted me, eyes bulging (he was a known drug user), picking up car engines on his own and putting them on the back of a transit van. I knew at this point that if I could not talk him round, I was due a whole lot of trouble, not to mention pain.

As it was on that occasion, luck was with me and there was no bloodshed. However it had made me realise that I did not really know how to defend myself, and I resolved to do something about that. A short time later I saw an advert for Wing Chun. After a demonstration, I was immediately taken with the directness of the system and have been training ever since.

I am still a police officer and as such strictly controlled as to when and how I should use force. On the face of it, it would seem that Wing Chun would not lend itself to this situation, where the ability to use short powerful punches, elbows and eye gouges are *definitely not* allowed except in extreme situations. Yet I have come to realise that some of the fundamental aspects of Wing Chun are very handy in my work.

By way of an example, I was recently sent to the home of a man who was compulsorily detained at a mental health institution. He had gone absent without permission, and I was warned that he was very unstable and violent. I arrived at the flat (yes, still with sweaty palms and a pounding heart) and found him there. I managed to get him to let me in and agree to come with me. However, he was still very volatile and kept going in and out of rooms and up and down the stairs. I felt that if I had tried to restrain him with handcuffs, it would have gone 'wobbly', as we say.

It was at this point that some of my recent training really began to work for me. Normally most people would try to keep a safe distance from a potential attacker, moving in as and when it seemed appropriate. Clearly this was something I could not do. Firstly because that is not how we are authorised to act, and secondly because of the confined space.

What I found myself doing was moving very close to the man, but not face-to-face. I positioned myself at his shoulder, virtually staring into his ear! I maintained this position and controlled his movement by stepping across him to deny him the chance to ever get into a stable position. I was also close enough to be touching him, so I could react to his slightest movements. Using this technique I was then able to shepherd him out and into the waiting transport without incident and without him realising what I was doing.

I have been practising this method in my Chi sau training, and have used it again in a similar incident to the above. Just by using the basic stance and moving in a strong and structured way we can, as Sun Tzu says, 'Attain the whole without fighting.' Alan asked me to write about using my Wing Chun in real situations, but when I come to think about it, I seem to have used it without using it.

Fighting without fighting perhaps?
If you have any interesting anecdotes about using Wing Chun in a real life situation (fighting or otherwise), that you wish to share, please write or email them to me at the address in the end of this book and I will consider publishing them in a future book, or on my website.
Alan Gibson

Contact us

The Wing Chun Federation was founded by Alan Gibson in 1990. The Federation's objective is to teach Wing Chun Kung Fu in a relaxed and accessible manner, where emphasis is placed on good technique and personal development. Wing Chun can be simply learnt by commitment and patience. Gender or physical size is of no consequence, and a high level of proficiency can be obtained quickly and with ease. We are a non-political organisation.

The Wing Chun Federation also runs regular self defence for women courses, where the student will learn the essentials of defending themselves against would be attackers, as well as how to avoid dangerous or uncomfortable confrontations where possible.

Representatives can be found in Southampton, Winchester, Portsmouth, Crowthorne, Isle of Wight and Bournemouth.

To contact the Wing Chun Federation to organise lessons or a seminar (no prior Wing Chun experience necessary), please write to:

Alan Gibson

The Wing Chun Federation,

12 Park Rd, Chandler's Ford, Eastleigh, Hants. SO53 2EU

Telephone: (U.K.) 023 8057 2084

email: alan@wingchun.org.uk

Or visit our web site at: www.wingchun.org.uk

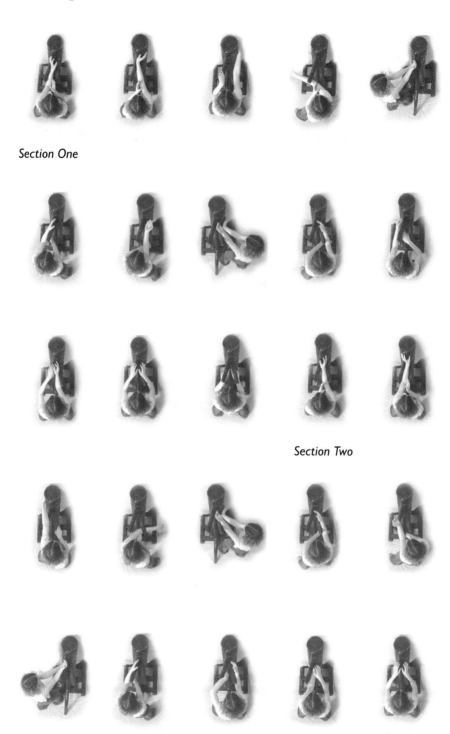

Section One

Section Two

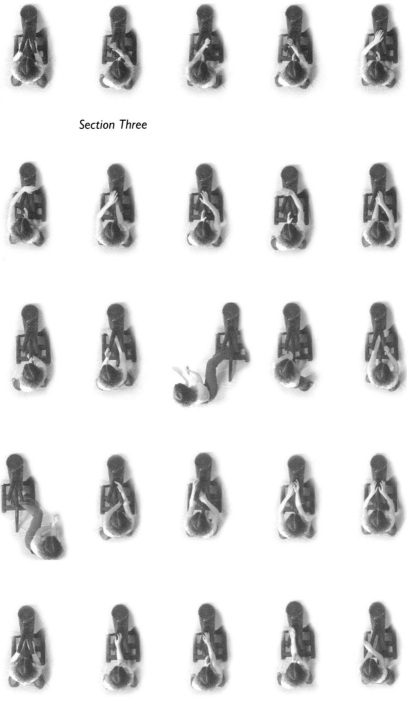

Section Three

Section Four

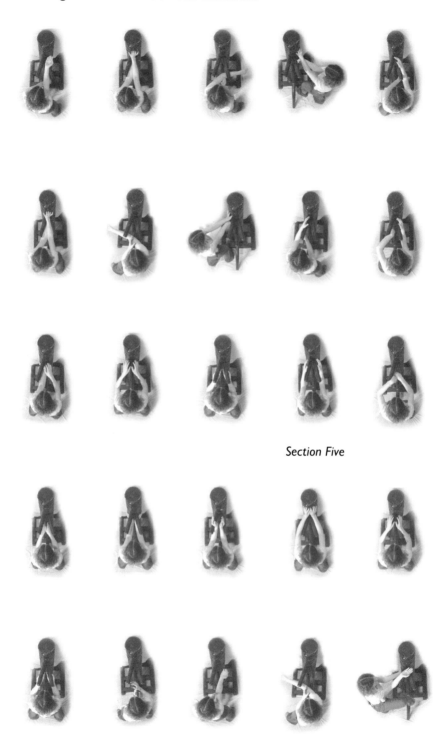

Section Five

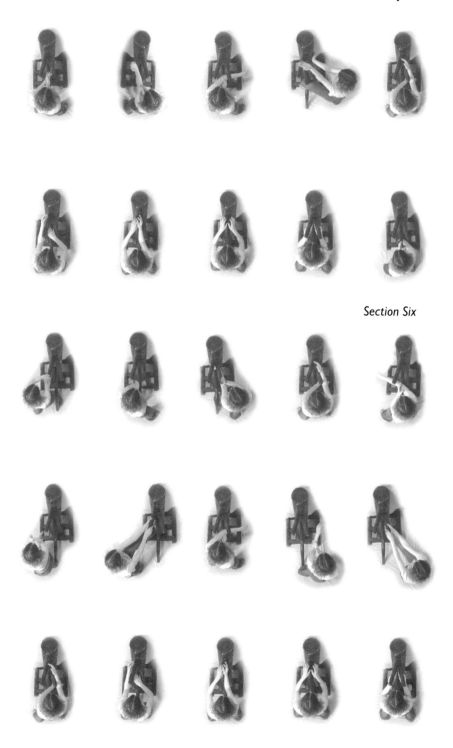

Section Six

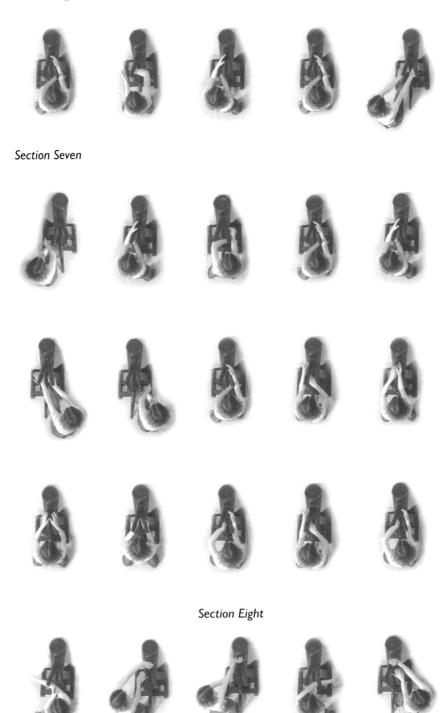

Section Seven

Section Eight

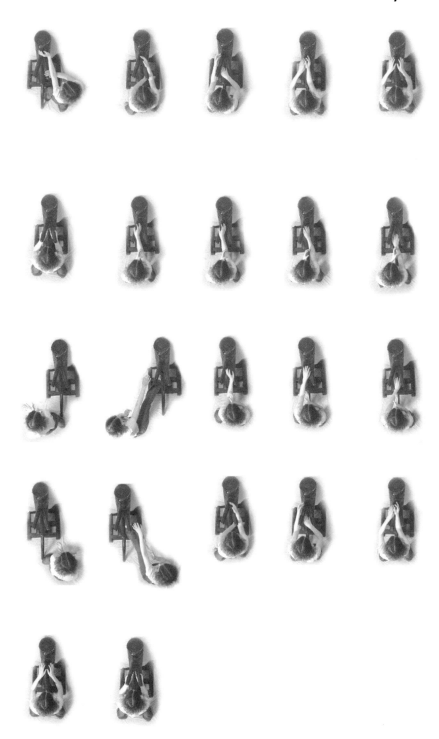

Wing Chun Form Posters

- With quality photography throughout, these posters will make remembering the forms far more easy.
- Ideal for the gym or home, these excellent aids make turning pages as you learn, a thing of the past.
- Presently available in poster format, Siu Lim Tao (first form) and Chum Kiu (second form).

Siu Lim Tao poster special price £6.00
Chum Kiu poster special price £6.00
Set of both posters special price £10.00
All prices include postage and packaging.
Send a cheque / postal order made out for **Alan Gibson**,
state which poster you require and include your address.

Send to:
The Wing Chun Federation
12 Park Rd
Chandlers Ford
Eastleigh
SO53 2EU

Only available in the U.K.   Please allow 28 days for delivery.

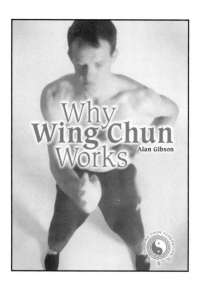

Why Wing Chun Works

The most popular and comprehensive Wing Chun book available in the UK. This in depth study systematically explains all the essential concepts, principles and basic training methods of the Wing Chun System. Why Wing Chun Works is the perfect training aid for anyone thinking about, or already studying, Wing Chun. It will also prove invaluable for other martial artists wishing to broaden their horizons.

Divided neatly into sections to facilitate the learning process and make cross-referencing simple, Why Wing Chun Works covers holistic health and philosophical argument and is clearly illustrated with photographs and diagrams. The book also has Siu Lim Tao, (Wing Chun's first form) completely demonstrated in numbered photographs.

Why Wing Chun Works £12.00
All prices include postage and packaging. Send a cheque / postal order made out for **Alan Gibson** and include your address.

Send to:
**The Wing Chun Federation, 12 Park Rd, Chandlers Ford
Eastleigh. SO53 2EU**

Only available in the U.K. Please allow 28 days for delivery.

Simple Thinking: Intelligent Fighters
(Why Wing Chun Works 2)

In the exiting sequel to his very popular first book 'Why Wing Chun Works', Alan Gibson explains how individual techniques and positions evolve as a result of the underlying Wing Chun concepts, and the forces we are likely to meet in combat.

Detailed photography, and clearly explained text, describe how fighting applications relate to Wing Chun theory. This book will undoubtedly become an invaluable reference work, both for Wing Chun practitioners and to all other thinking martial artists. The book also has Chum Kiu, (Wing Chun's second form) completely demonstrated in numbered photographs.

Simple Thinking: Intelligent Fighters (Why Wing Chun Works 2) £12.00
All prices include postage and packaging.
Send a cheque / postal order made out for **Alan Gibson** and include your address.
Send to:
The Wing Chun Federation
12 Park Rd
Chandlers Ford
Eastleigh
SO53 2EU

Only available in the U.K. Please allow 28 days for delivery.

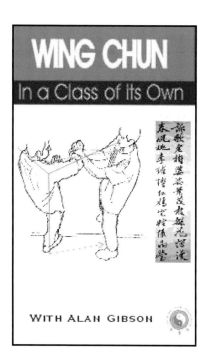

Wing Chun In a Class of its Own (VHS Video)

In this refreshing, and entertaining look at the Wing Chun system, Alan Gibson guides the viewer through all the main drills and theories of the system. The first two forms and the dummy are demonstrated; the concepts are then backed up with explosive applications. This excellent 45 minute film is digitally shot and edited, using several different locations.

Wing Chun In a Class of its Own £19.95
All prices include postage and packaging.
Send a cheque / postal order made out for **Alan Gibson** and include your address.
Send to:
The Wing Chun Federation
12 Park Rd
Chandlers Ford
Eastleigh
SO53 2EU

Only available in the U.K. Please allow 28 days for delivery.